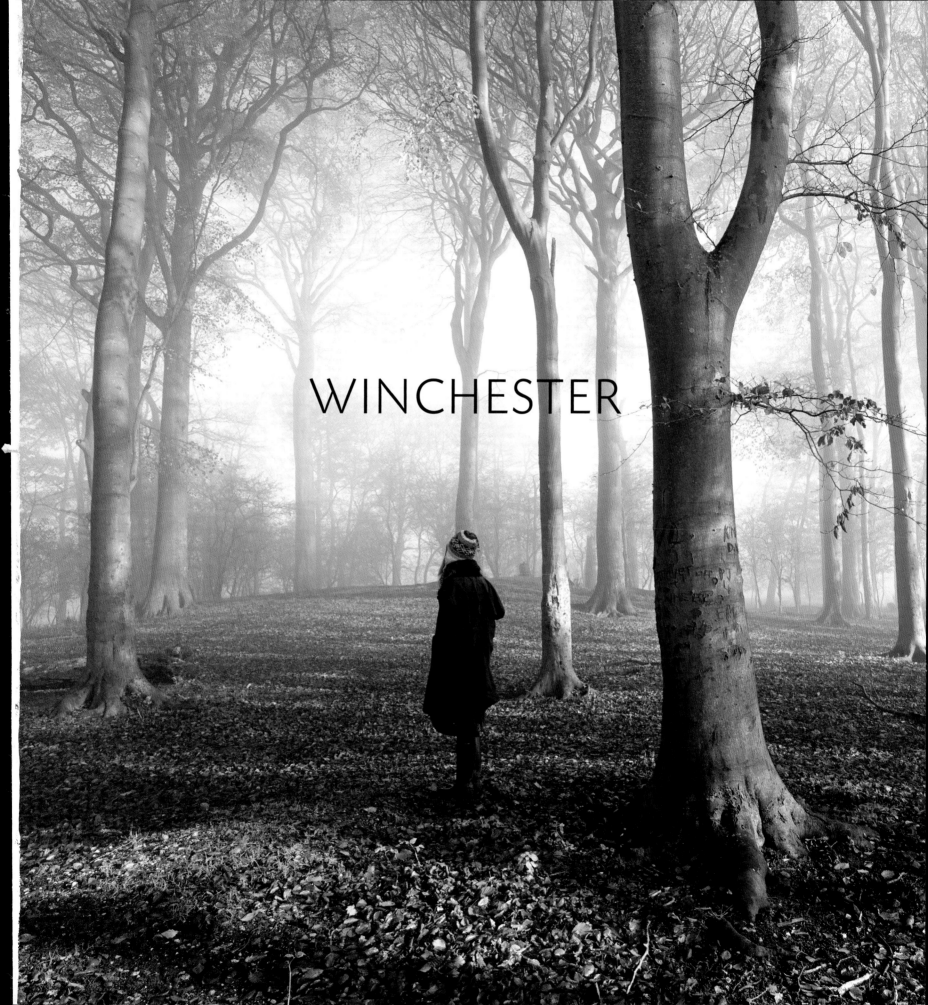

WINCHESTER

WINCHESTER
Chris Caldicott

FRANCES LINCOLN LIMITED

PUBLISHERS

Frances Lincoln Ltd
www.franceslincoln.com

Winchester
Copyright © Frances Lincoln Limited 2012
Text and photographs copyright © Chris Caldicott 2012

First Frances Lincoln edition 2012

British Library Cataloguing-in-Publication data
A catalogue record for this book is available from the British Library.

ISBN: 978-0-7112-3326-3

Printed and bound in China

9 8 7 6 5 4 3 2 1

PAGE 1 The copse of beech trees on the top of St Catherine's Hill on a misty
spring morning
PAGES 2–3 The Itchen flowing through the water meadows on a frosty winter
morning
BELOW Winchester Cathedral towering above the tree line in early summer
PAGES 6–7 The College Chapel and the ruins of Wolvesey Castle seen from
St Giles's Hill in autumn

CONTENTS

INTRODUCTION

Visiting Winchester for the first time is like finding a hidden jewel in the Hampshire countryside. Located on the slopes and along the bed of a picturesque and fertile chalk valley watered by the River Itchen, Winchester is an ancient city of great historic integrity that offers simultaneously rural serenity and dynamic urban diversity. Its plethora of well-preserved iconic architecture and vibrant traditions, combined with a topography that has ensured that swathes of unspoilt countryside penetrate right into the ancient settlement and modern city, make it quite unique.

Remnants of every period of Winchester's rich history can still be seen scattered around the contemporary city and the Itchen valley. To describe Winchester as a city is rather misleading, for although its cathedral and crown courts may well give it city status, in reality Winchester is no more than a small town. Much of the historic centre is intact, and as evocative as that of any medieval town in Europe, and although modern suburbs have spread up both sides of the valley, houses are still outnumbered by trees and urban sprawl by open spaces. As the flood plain of the Itchen, the wide valley floor remains free of any development, an idyllic patchwork of water meadows, farmland and woodland. There are viewpoints around the valley where the only man-made structures visible above the treetops are the towers of the Norman cathedral and the medieval churches of St Cross and the College, with nothing but open countryside beyond them.

This unusual combination of rural and urban environment gives the changing character of each season through the year particular relevance in Winchester. Even the bleakest winter days of violent storms and driving rain have an appealing drama to them. Spring brings meadows of wildflowers and fabulous blossoms right in the city centre; on the hottest days of summer, the cool, fast-flowing clear waters of the Itchen and the breezes on the summit of St Catherine's Hill offer instant relief; and autumn is a feast of colour and falling leaves among the narrow lanes and open spaces. This book celebrates in images a year in the life of Winchester.

HISTORY

Remnants of a Bronze Age settlement, on the summit of St Catherine's Hill on the eastern side of the Itchen valley, are the earliest evidence of a permanent population in the area. The earthwork walls of a hill fort can still be clearly seen encircling the hill. An Iron Age settlement was later established on the slope of Oram's Arbour on the other side of the valley.

The Romans invaded Britain in AD 43 and by AD 70 they had built the city Venta Belgarum or 'Market of the Belgae' on the site of the Arbour, and were running it as a provincial capital. Still today the arrow-straight Roman roads they built run from Winchester north-west to Andover, north to Basingstoke, south-east to Porchester and west to Salisbury.

By the third century stone walls had been built to keep rebellious hordes of ancient Britons at bay, and Venta Belgarum had been extended far beyond Oram's Arbour eastwards all the way to the west bank of the Itchen. The walled city, which included a forum and temple, could only be entered by way of six fortified gateways. Nothing remains of the North, East, South and Durn Gates, but later versions of the West and King's Gates (Westgate and Kingsgate) are still important parts of the city.

Venta Belgarum became the fifth largest town in Roman Britain. A superb section of Roman mosaic pavement from this time is on display in the City Museum. This was a short taste of early importance for the town that would one day be known as Winchester. However, by the fourth century Roman Britain, along with the rest of the Empire, was slipping into decline and by AD 410 Venta Belgarum had been abandoned.

During the establishment of the Saxon kingdoms Belgarum was little more than the abode of insignificant local landlord rulers and self-declared monarchs. However, in the seventh century, following the defeat of King Atwald of Wight by King Cenwalh of Wessex, the city, under the new name of Wintonceastre, was recognized as capital of the kingdom of Wessex.

It was Cenwalh who, in 648, built Winchester's first version of a Christian cathedral, now known as the Old Minster. This was to be an important religious centre, its status significantly enhanced by the fact that it soon became the burial place for Wessex kings, including the most important of them all, King Alfred the Great in 899.

The twelfth-century Westgate: one of the two surviving city gates

One of the biggest players in the history of Winchester was a ninth-century cleric named Swithun, reportedly at one time tutor to Alfred, who became Bishop of the Old Minster. Around 850 Swithun increased the city's accessibility by ordering the construction of the first bridge over the Itchen (on the site where City Bridge now stands), and he extended the Roman walls substantially to increase the city's size. Historically more important than these tangible achievements, though, was his canonization as a saint and – especially – his reputation as a miracle-worker. Visiting his sacred remains in search of a cure for all manner of afflictions became a motivation for pilgrimages to Winchester for centuries.

The most famous of Swithun's reputed miracles was the restoration of a woman's basket of broken eggs, maliciously destroyed by a bad-tempered workman on Swithun's own bridge. Today, however, St Swithun is best known for his capacity as a weather prophet. In characteristic pious humility he is said to have desired to be buried outside the Old Minster so that 'the foot of passers-by, and the rainwater from the eaves, could fall upon his grave'. When he died in 862 his wish came true. His body remained here for more than a hundred years and legend has it that from the day his remains were moved inside the Old Minster, 15 July 971, it rained for forty days as a mark of his displeasure. Despite controversy about the accuracy of this tale, St Swithun's day, 15 July, is still celebrated as a church feast day, and the saying endures:

St Swithun's day if thou dost rain
For forty days it will remain.
St Swithun's day if thou be fair
For forty days t'will rain nae mare.

The journey to pay homage to the saint's remains became a major pilgrimage for Christians from all over northern Europe, many stopping off here on their way to Canterbury. A well-maintained network of footpaths still connects Winchester to Canterbury via the South Downs Way; and many ancient trails, footpaths and pilgrimage routes around Winchester are still designated as rights of way on Ordnance Survey maps. But only faint traces remain of the original Pilgrims' Way (taken by Henry II in 1174 in penance for the murder of Thomas Becket), which linked the two cathedral cities.

Most of the urban street plans and system of rural waterways, canals and sluices seen in Winchester today date back to the time of Alfred the Great, crowned here in 871. Alfred also greatly strengthened the fortifications of the city, as well as building defences along the English coasts. This was very necessary, as threats to the island nation now came from across the North Sea, in the form of Viking attacks.

The Anglo-Saxons were pushed to the brink of collapse by the marauding Vikings but Alfred was able to unite the nation – previously separated into separate Anglo-Saxon domains – and repel the invaders. It was through Alfred's efforts that a united England became possible. As great a scholar and statesman as he was a soldier, he was also responsible for initiating academic institutions and law reforms to improve the quality of life of his people, and he is venerated to this day as a national hero. He is even regarded by some as a saint, although he was never canonized. The Anglican Church still honours him with a feast day on 26 October. In 1901, to mark (albeit two years late) the millenary of Alfred's death in 899. a large bronze statue made by Hamo Thornycroft was erected in the Winchester Broadway. The day it was unveiled was declared a public holiday and a huge crowd of Wintonians gathered to celebrate the event.

In 901, Alfred's son, Edward the Elder, founded a New Minster just north of the old one. Edward's son Athelstan reconquered the remaining territories under Viking control. and became King of England – and so Winchester became the capital of England.

In 964 Bishop Ethelwold reformed the Old Minster into a Benedictine monastery known as St Swithun's Priory. Then in the 970s he built a monastic palace at Wolvesey, where the bishop and monks who ran the New Minster lived.

Late Anglo-Saxon England was politically very volatile, with the Anglo-Saxons and the Vikings battling each other and among themselves. However, kings of England were still crowned and buried in Winchester. In 1035 King Canute was buried in the Old Minster and in 1043 Edward the Confessor was crowned in the cathedral. Less than twenty years later William the Conqueror turned up; and changed England's history. After all Alfred's tireless efforts and military skill, which had kept England safe from invasion from the Nordic hordes during his rule, his descendants surrendered almost without a fight to the armies of Normandy who had sailed over the Channel from France. In 1066 William was symbolically handed the keys to Winchester and its abbey.

These Norman invaders built a castle on the west side of the Itchen valley, and a palace that occupied the area of the city now known as the Square. And in 1079, on the site of Cenwalh's Anglo-Saxon Old Minster, Bishop Walkelin, William's appointee, began work began on what was to become the longest and one of the most architecturally ambitious cathedrals in all of Europe. The magnificent Norman Winchester Cathedral still dominates the city nearly a thousand years later, although it has been regularly added to and altered throughout its long history – first in 1107, less than thirty years after it was built, when the tower of Walkelin's cathedral collapsed. At the time the disaster was blamed on the unpopular King William Rufus, whose remains were buried under the tower. But the tower was rebuilt in 1202 and it still stands today.

Following the Norman Conquest Winchester retained much of its significance. It was here that William the Conqueror's famous record of the state of the realm was complied. Everything gathered was sent to Winchester's royal court, where the information was recorded and edited. It was not until 1180 that this record was named the Domesday Book. Previously it was referred to as the 'King's Roll' or the 'Winchester Roll'.

Although during this time London's importance was growing – by the end of the twelfth century it would be the nation's capital – the kingdom's royal treasury remained in Winchester until the reign of Henry II. And between 1087 (William the Conqueror's death) and 1154 (Henry II's accession to the throne), anyone hoping for acceptance as monarch had to be the first to reach Winchester. William Rufus, on his father the Conqueror's death, raced here at once from Rouen. On Rufus's death his brother Henry did the same; two days after his arrival in Winchester he was crowned Henry I. The importance of being first to Winchester was never more apparent than in 1135, when Henry I died. Although he had named his daughter Matilda as his successor, it was her cousin Stephen of Blois who reached the city first. Stephen took control of the treasury and hastily arranged for his coronation in Winchester Cathedral. What followed was years of civil war (in 1141 Winchester came under siege) until November 1153, when a peace treaty was made at Winchester. It was agreed that Henry, Matilda's son, was Stephen's heir. A year later Stephen was dead and Henry II was on the throne.

In 1129 Henry of Blois – great-grandson of William the Conqueror and younger brother of the soon-to-be King of England, Stephen – was elected as Bishop of Winchester. At somewhere between twenty-eight and thirty he was very young for the post of Bishop of the richest see in the country, but he was to play an active role in the history, not only of Winchester, but of England. Throughout the battle for the throne both Stephen and Matilda would strive to gain his support.

He also made a considerable contribution to the fabric of Winchester. He oversaw the reconstruction of the Anglo-Saxon bishop's palace of Wolvesey Castle. And in 1136 he also built a substantial hospital as accommodation for elderly gentlemen, and, in its grounds, a beautiful church. The Hospital and Church of St Cross still stand today, dramatically dominating the southern section of the water meadows along the Itchen.

Westgate was rebuilt in the twelfth century and further fortified: a portcullis was added, and openings were made below the parapet for pouring boiling lead and oil on potential attackers. In the sixteenth century it became a debtors' prison and today it is one of Winchester's many museums. The Tudor ceiling was decorated to celebrate the marriage of Queen Mary to Philip of Spain at the Cathedral in 1554.

In 1235 Henry III – often referred to as Henry of Winchester, as the city was his birthplace and a place he loved to visit – modernized the Norman castle built in the time of William the Conqueror, adding the Great Hall. Although most of the Castle was destroyed in 1302 – by a fire which nearly killed Edward I and his wife, Margaret – the Great Hall miraculously survived intact and remains one of the finest medieval buildings still standing in England. It is famous as the location of 'King Arthur's Round Table', which has hung in the hall for over six hundred years. The table actually dates from the thirteenth century, so was made long after Arthur supposedly lived – although some like to promote the myth that it was made by the wizard Merlin. It was originally undecorated but was later painted for Henry VIII, depicting Arthur with Henry's face and in Tudor robes, surrounded by the names of the legendary Knights of the Round Table.

In the late fourteenth century the remarkable William of Wykeham was Bishop of Winchester. Wykeham is considered by many the outstanding hero of Winchester' history. He was responsible for radical improvements to the Cathedral, which have lasted to the present day. He founded the still extant and oldest continuously run public school in England, Winchester College (whose students are referred to as Wykehamists). Born a peasant in 1324, by the time of his death in 1404 Wykeham was one of the richest men in England. His motto, 'manners makyth man', is still used by the College and the other great institution he founded, New College in Oxford. Most of his architectural legacy in Winchester survived the ravages of Henry VIII's reformation, Parliamentarian sacking and civil war.

Upon Wykeham's death Bishop Henry Beaufort – who was half-brother to Henry IV – was translated from the see of Lincoln to the much grander see of Winchester. Beaufort became a key figure in England's history. He was godfather to Henry VI and played a leading role in the young King's regency. In 1426 he was made a cardinal.

In 1446 Beaufort rebuilt the Hospital of St Cross as an Almshouse of Noble Poverty. A year later he died at Wolvesey Castle and was buried in the Cathedral.

During the Middle Ages the wool trade and cloth-making dominated the city's economy. This was a period of mixed fortunes, when some of Winchester's finest iconic buildings – many of which have lasted to the present day – were constructed, but also, sadly, when much of its past was destroyed.

Every September a great fair was held on St Giles's Hill, attracting merchants from all over Britain and Continental Europe. Most of Winchester's timber-framed buildings, like those still found in Canon Street, date from this period; they were often constructed from reclaimed ships' timbers brought up-river from the docks of Southampton and Portsmouth. The oldest of them still standing is the Old Chesil Rectory (now a restaurant), built in 1450.

By the Tudor period Winchester's history had become much less eventful; although in 1538 Henry VIII's reformation saw the dissolution of Winchester's three monasteries and the demolition of St Swithun's shrine in the Cathedral.

In the early sixteenth century several water mills were constructed in Winchester to harness the power of the fast-flowing Itchen. One of them, known as City Mill, bequeathed to the city by Mary Tudor by royal charter in 1554, rebuilt in 1744 and more recently restored by the National Trust, is still in full working order and open to the public. In the early twentieth century it was leased to the Youth Hostel Association: guests were offered spartan accommodation and obliged to wash in the race of the Itchen. The Winchester Ladies' Swimming Club also used it as a place to dip in the river, clinging to

ropes in the fast current and protected by the structure of the mill from any prying eyes.

In 1587 Peter Symonds, a wealthy textile merchant, bequeathed a large sum of money in his will to the creation of Christ's Hospital almshouse in Symonds Street for the maintenance of six old men, a matron and four boys. Due to issues with the will, this was not built until 1607.

Parliamentarian soldiers implementing one of Cromwell's puritanical purges violated the sanctity of the Cathedral in 1642. Soldiers on horseback defiled the high altar, smashed medieval stained-glass windows, and scattered holy manuscripts and the bones of Saxon saints, kings and bishops as though they were common trash. It is believed that even worse desecration was prevented by the timely arrival on the scene of a Parliamentarian colonel named Fiennes, who by chance was an old Wykehamist and who, standing with a drawn sword, protected the chantry of the founder of his alma mater from the iconoclastic tendencies of his own troopers. Again in 1645, Parliamentarian soldiers beseiged Winchester Castle, expelled its Royalist occupants and demolished everything except the Great Hall, which once again survived.

Near the Great Hall Charles II commissioned an extravagant palace designed by Sir Christopher Wren as a copy of the palace at Versailles. It was not finished before the King's death and it burned down in 1894. Where it once stood, there are the elegant red-brick buildings of the Peninsular Terrace Barracks. These are now partly residential and the location of Winchester's five military museums. A bronze statue of Queen Victoria, commissioned to celebrate her Golden Jubilee in 1897, was installed in a corner of the Great Hall. In 1986 the medieval garden was reconstructed behind the Hall, using a fourteenth-century manuscript illustration as a guide. It was named Queen Eleanor's Garden for the wife of Henry II, Queen Eleanor of Provence, and her daughter-in-law Queen Eleanor of Castile, wife of Edward I. It was opened by the late Queen Mother.

Ironically the most devastating period of destruction of the city's antiquities occurred relatively recently, when post-war city planners allowed much of the old town to be demolished and replaced by such architectural horrors as the Brooks Shopping Centre and the police headquarters. Despite this and the regrettable destruction of Twyford Down to accommodate the M3 motorway in the 1980s, Winchester remains one of the most well preserved historic cities in the world – and one of the most idyllic.

Fromond's Chantry, Winchester College

'King Arthur's Round Table' in the Great Hall

Peninsular Barracks Square, rebuilt in 1804 after a fire destroyed King's House

The house at 8 College Street where Jane Austen lived just before her death in 1817

The eighteenth-century
City Mill

The Cathedral
and Close

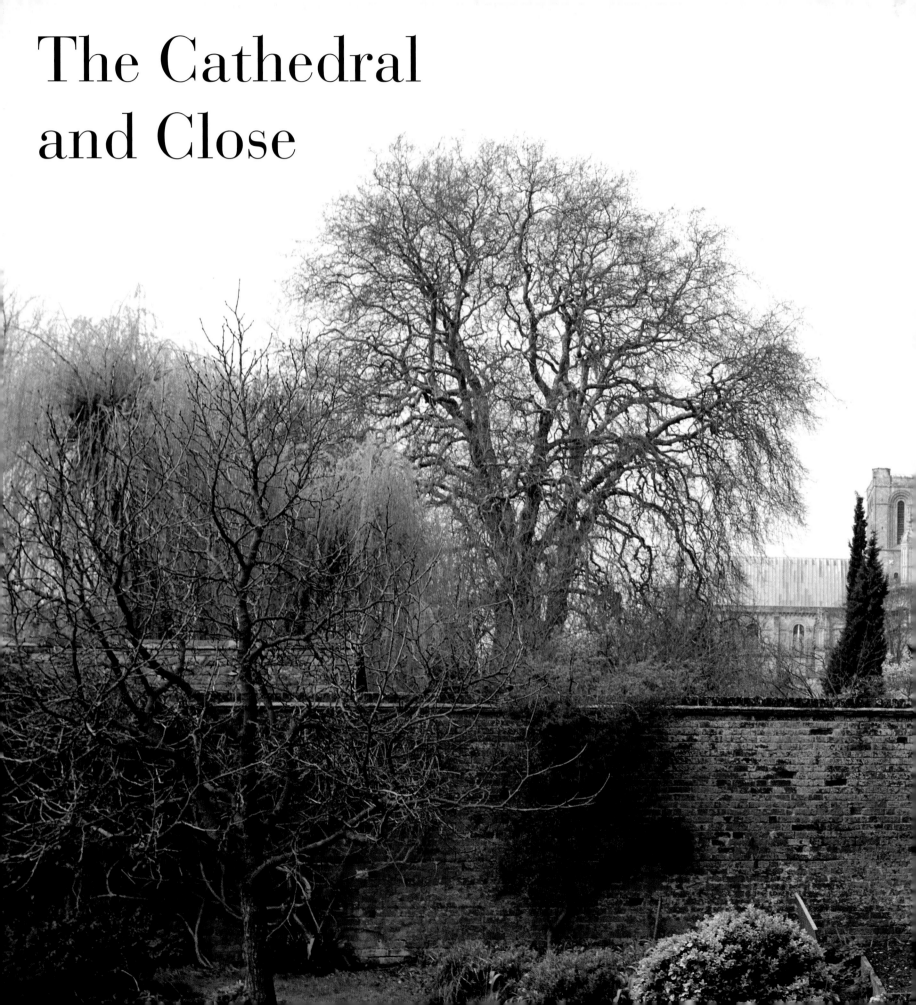

THE CATHEDRAL AND CLOSE

Any year in the life of Winchester Cathedral is naturally dictated by the ecclesiastical calendar. There are regular services here every Sunday and several special ones through the year, including Remembrance Day, Law Lords' Day and the midnight mass at Christmas, all enhanced by the singing of the wonderful Winchester Cathedral Choir, including the boy choristers from the Pilgrims' School. The Cathedral is particularly spectacular at Christmas, when a festive market and ice rink are set up in the Close.

Today the Cathedral forms part of a walled city within modern Winchester. The Cathedral Close is only accessible to the public via the Cathedral itself and three gateways, all of which are locked every night at 10 p.m. Many of the city's most historically significant and iconic buildings are located in the protected sanctuary of the Close. These include the thirteenth-century vaulted-porch Deanery, the twelfth-century flint-rubble-walled Pilgrims' Hall with the oldest surviving hammer-beamed roof in England, the arched remains of the Norman Chapter House and the stunning sixteenth-century timber-framed Cheyney Court and Priory Stables, the former once the bishop's courthouse and the latter now part of the Pilgrims' School.

William of Wykeham's improvements to the Cathedral, which included refashioning the nave in soaring Perpendicular style, kept it structurally sound until the beginning of the twentieth century, when it was realized that the east end of the building, supported by beech logs on marshy ground, was in danger of collapse caused by subsidence. The only solution was to replace all the rotting timbers with concrete. This was achieved by the extraordinary efforts of a deep-sea diver named William Walker, who spent more than five years submerged for six hours a day in total darkness at depths of up to 6 metres/20 feet under the foundations. His success in saving the building is commemorated by a bronze statue in the Cathedral's retrochoir, which was built in the thirteenth century to accommodate the pilgrims visiting the shrine of St Swithun. On the west side of the retrochoir is an impressive collection of painted icons above the 'Holy Hole', a low tunnel which allowed pilgrims to crawl beneath a platform on which Swithun's bones were displayed, in order to get close to their curative powers. To the east is the ornate Lady Chapel.

The Cathedral has many other hidden treasures. Up a flight of stairs in the south transept is the library, where the twelfth-century Winchester Bible is on permanent display. Written in the hand of a single scribe and exquisitely illustrated, this is a priceless example of the work of the renowned Winchester School.

There are also exhibits in the library of the few remaining statues saved from the Cathedral's Great Screen, which was destroyed by the iconoclastic Elizabethan Bishop Horne, who ordered all the original statues of this magnificent fifteenth-century reredos to be smashed to pieces. (The statues seen in their place today are perfectly acceptable nineteenth-century replacements.)

On a wall of the north transept is a fabulous stained-glass window designed by Edward Burne-Jones and made in William Morris's workshop. On the north side of the nave is the twelfth-century font, made of black Tournai marble with benevolent acts performed by St Nicholas carved on its sides. One shows him providing bags of gold as marriage dowries for the daughters of an impoverished nobleman, another resurrecting three young men slain by an evil landlord. Nearby is the grave of Jane Austen and a brass wall tablet celebrating her life.

Among the most intimate delights of the Cathedral is the small Fisherman's Chapel on the eastern side of the south transept. Izaak Walton, the seventeenth-century fisherman and author of *The Compleat Angler*, is buried here. One section of the beautiful stained glass above the oak altar depicts him reading on the banks of the River Itchen below St Catherine's Hill, with the motto 'Study to be Quiet'.

A small doorway in the north transept leads down to the Norman crypt, which regularly floods when the Itchen is in spate, sometimes reaching as high as the thighs of the impressive Anthony Gormley statue, *Sound II*, of a life-size standing man. Here (when it is dry enough), may also be seen a collection of ancient statues and a stone coffin that is thought to have been the final coffin of St Swithun.

Most impressive of all is the climb up the Cathedral tower, winding steeply up tiny, narrow stairways and gravity-defying elevated walkways to the bell tower and roof. There are stunning views from the top over the Cathedral precincts, the College, the Wolvesey Castle ruins, the city, St Catherine's Hill and the water meadows, all the way to St Cross.

PAGES 17–18 The Cathedral in early spring, from a walled garden in Colebrook Street
LEFT The Cathedral in summer

The Cathedral in spring

The Cathedral in autumn

The Cathedral in winter

PAGES 24–25 Inside Winchester Cathedral
TOP LEFT Fedorov's *Iconostasis* on the retroquire
BOTTOM LEFT St Swithun's memorial shrine
RIGHT The nave

Sound II, statue by Antony Gormley, in the Norman crypt

Looking through the Priory Gate entrance
to the Cathedral Close at Priory Stables,
now part of Pilgrims' School

The stone balustrade and statue at
the north entrance to the Close

LEFT The Deanery and Cathedral from
Cathedral Close
RIGHT The Cathedral through spring blossom

Church House, Cathedral Close

The sixteenth-century towering gables of Cheyney Court, where the Bishop once held court over the suburbs of the Soke, beyond the city walls; and Prior's Gate, opening on to Kingsgate

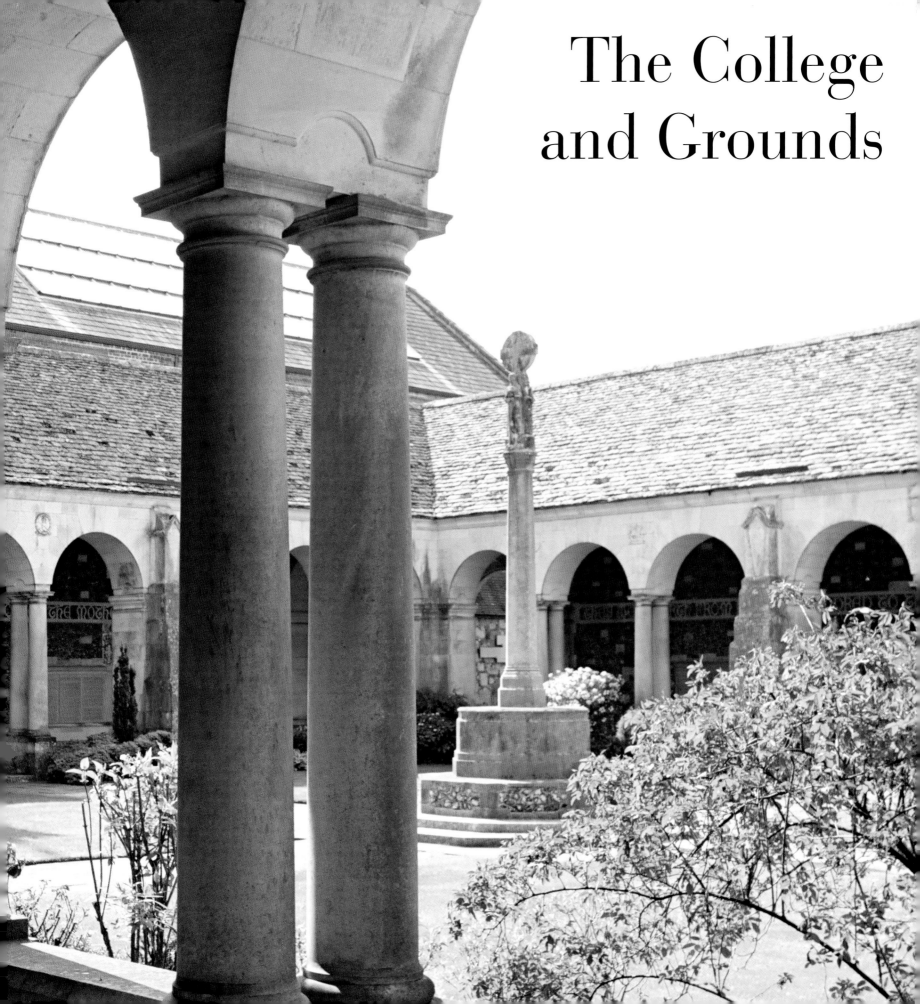

The College
and Grounds

THE COLLEGE AND GROUNDS

William of Wykeham, Bishop of Winchester from 1366, started constructing Winchester College in 1382, with the intention of providing an academic institution to prepare seventy needy scholars for his recently founded New College in Oxford. His aim was to create a new generation of educated priests in church and government to replace those lost during the Black Death. To support the scholars he further provided for two masters, a warden, ten fellows, three chaplains, sixteen choristers and three lay clerks to administer the College and provide religious services and music in the Chapel.

Today seventy scholars are still housed in the medieval buildings of Wykeham's original college and a further 630 boys aged between thirteen and eighteen, referred to as 'Commoners', live in ten designated boarding houses beyond the campus, located around the Kingsgate area of the old city. Public access to the College's architectural heritage is offered on very well guided tours. Highlights include the Chamber Court (a quadrangle enclosed by the fellows' and scholars' chambers, which the boys once used as a washing place); the beautiful Gothic College Chapel, consecrated in 1394, which has a stunning early example of an ornate wooden vaulted roof, and lavish stained-glass windows; the scholars' dining room, which is still in use; the complete quadrangle of stone cloisters surrounding the Fromond's Chantry; and the evocative War Cloister. There are also many intriguing details to see. The prolific graffiti include some that date back to medieval times – and also Trollope's name carved on a bannister. There are many finely carved heads on the sides of buildings, including one of a blue-eyed boy above the Porter's Gate.

The College year is built around term times. During Common Time (spring term) the boys play a game unique to Winchester College known as 'Win:Co:Fo:' or 'Winkies'. This has elements of football and rugby in it, but is not really much like either; it is and played on a pitch delimited lengthwise by canvas netting and posts threaded with heavy rope. Cricket is the game of Cloister Time (summer term) and the College first eleven, known as 'Lords', plays an annual match against Eton, held at the two schools alternately.

The unusual names for terms and games reflect the fact that the College has a vocabulary all of its own, a tradition known as 'Notions', which new boys are taught in their first term, after which they refer, for instance, to prep as 'toytime' and the desks it is done on as 'toyes', while a bicycle is a 'bogle'.

PAGES 36–37 The War Cloister of Winchester College in spring
LEFT The College Chapel tower, with St Catherine's Hill beyond, in summer
ABOVE A detail of a door at the College

LEFT
TOP The College in winter
BOTTOM LEFT The statue of
the blue-eyed boy, above the
Porter's Gate
BOTTOM RIGHT A wall statue

RIGHT Statues in elevated
alcoves on a wall of the College

The College grounds in winter

A branch of the Itchen flowing
through the College grounds east
of the Chapel, on a spring morning

FAR LEFT The cricket pavilion
LEFT The College Sick House
OPPOSITE BELOW The College Meads and the Science Building

RIGHT Boys playing the Win:Co:Fo game in Common Time
BELOW LEFT Trollope's name, carved on a bannister
BELOW RIGHT Nineteenth-century graffiti in the School Building

The Chapel

A stained-glass window in the Chapel

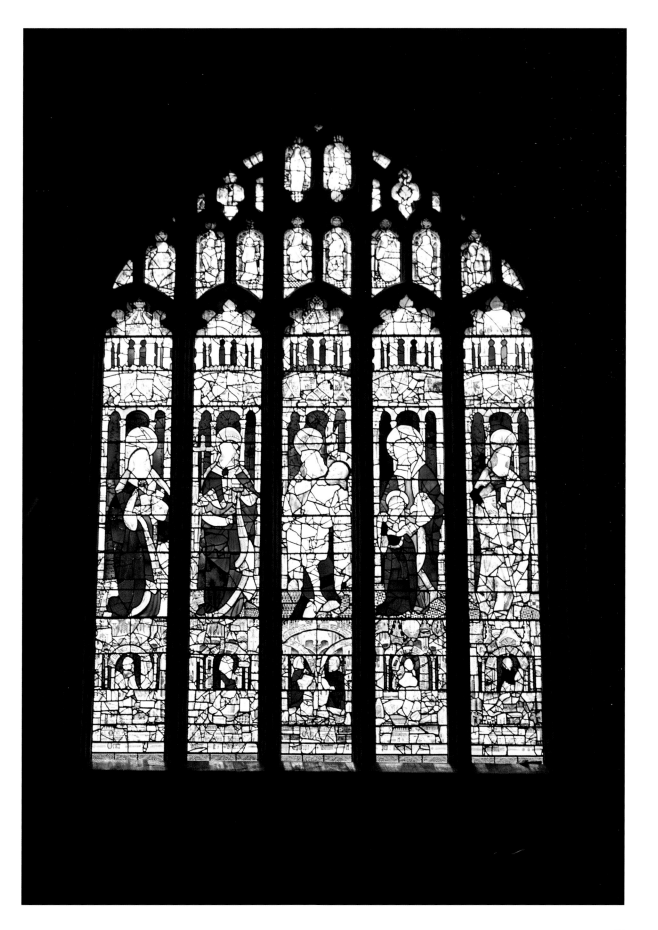

The Old Cloisters around
Fromond's Chantry

The Dining Hall

The War Cloister, built in 1924 as a memorial to Wykehamists who died in World War I

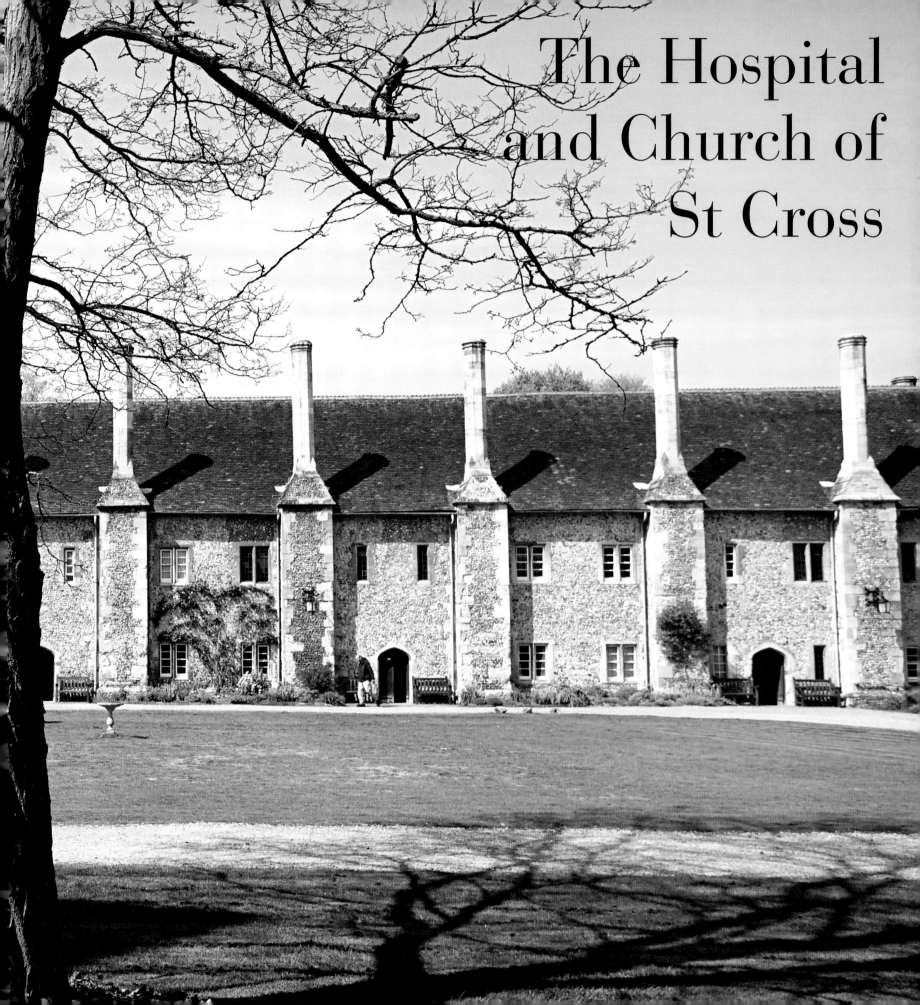

The Hospital and Church of St Cross

THE HOSPITAL AND CHURCH OF ST CROSS

The Hospital of St Cross was founded by Henry of Blois in 1136 and still stands today: a wonderful stately pile rising from the fertile meadows bordering the banks of the Itchen in a peaceful suburb south of the city. Blois decreed that the building should provide support for 'thirteen poor men, feeble and so reduced in strength that they can hardly or not at all support themselves without another's aid'. They were also to be provided with 'garments and beds suitable to their infirmities, good wheate bread daily of the weight of 5 marks, and three dishes at dinner and one at supper, suitable to the day, and drink of good stuff'. The hospital complex included the 'Hundred Men's Hall' where a hundred local poor men were to be served dinner every day. The fine Transitional Norman church in the hospital grounds – which would have been built with a thatched roof – was used as a point of departure for crusaders on their way to the Holy Land.

In 1446 Cardinal Beaufort refounded St Cross as an Almshouse of Noble Poverty and provider of a 'wayfarer's dole' of bread and ale for pilgrims. Today a mug of ale and piece of bread are handed out at the Porter's Gate, included in the entry ticket to the site. The hospital is still home to twenty-five brothers, who live in self-contained flats in Beaufort's original tall-chimneyed lodgings on the west of the quadrangle. Those of the Blois foundation wear black gowns and a Jerusalem Cross, while the Beaufort clan dress in red robes with a cardinal's badge.

St Cross is a visual treat at any time of the year, in views looking west from St Catherine's Hill, north from Bushfield Down or across the water meadows. The exterior can be seen at any time from a riverside pathway that passes it to the east and enters an avenue of limes on its way through the farmland around it. There is a small café just inside the main gate but all the best bits, including the the Compton (or Master's) Garden, the Norman church, the old kitchens and the Brethren's Hall, lie beyond the Porter's Gate. The Compton Garden, named after Henry Compton, who was Master of St Cross between 1667 and 1676 and later went on to be Bishop of London, is a triumph of garden design, using plants imported from the New World in Compton's time. There is a tulip tree that was planted in the garden to commemorate a visit by the Queen Mother in 1986. Every year in June a traditional fête is held in the garden and grounds.

PAGES 52–53 The Brothers' Quarters at the Hospital of St Cross
LEFT St Cross from the water meadows on a winter morning
RIGHT St Cross from St Catherine's Hill

St Cross on a misty autumn day

The Church of St Cross and the Compton Garden
at midsummer

The Brothers' Quarters
and the Church of St
Cross from the south, in
early spring

LEFT The Choir; CENTRE Chevron mouldings in the chapel; RIGHT The vaulted ceiling

The kitchens

Wolvesey Castle
and Palace

WOLVESEY CASTLE AND PALACE

There has been an ecclesiastical building on the site of Wolvesey Palace since Anglo-Saxon times. Wolvesey Castle survived the early days after the Norman Conquest as a modest residence where the Bishop lived with a community of monks; then in the twelfth century it was substantially extended by Bishop Henry of Blois. The magnificent ruins seen today are mostly from this period.

When Henry of Blois became Bishop of Winchester in 1129, the residence consisted of a large hall block (the 'west hall'). As a prince of both the Church and the state, he must have felt that a grander residence was called for. He added the 'east hall', a keep, a defensive tower and two gatehouses. He also installed one of the earliest known medieval examples of piped water and plumbing. Between 1141 and 1154 the kitchens were built to prepare feasts for the Bishop's household and guests. In 1403 they were put to good use at Henry IV's wedding, where they served such delicacies as cygnets, venison, rabbits, partridges, quail and snipe. By 1170 the Palace was surrounded by a moat and arranged around an inner courtyard.

Wolvesey was just one of many grand palaces in Hampshire belonging to the Winchester bishops, who spent much of their time travelling between them in the course of their diocesan duties. They also derived great wealth from the rents of vast landholdings. Their yearly accounts were documented on large parchment manuscripts that were rolled into pipe shapes. These rolls, known as the Winchester Pipe Rolls, are now held in the County Record Office.

Although subsequent bishops carried out various repairs and alterations, the twelfth-century version of Wolvesey Palace was still up and running in 1554, when Mary Tudor and King Philip of Spain stayed here during their wedding ceremony and celebrations at the Cathedral. But when Bishop Morley built his new palace next door, just over a hundred years later, the old one was plundered for building materials, then left to fall into ruin.

The official residence of the present-day Bishop of Winchester is a baroque palace set in beautiful manicured grounds facing the Cathedral, just west of the old one. During the summer months open-air theatre productions are held among the evocative ruins of Wolvesey.

PAGES 66–69 The ruins of the old Wolvesey Castle and Palace

LEFT Wolvesey Palace
BELOW The coat of arms above the door of the Palace

Wolvesey Palace and the ruins of the Castle

An ornate urn in the grounds of the Palace

The Water Meadows and St Catherine's Hill

THE WATER MEADOWS AND ST CATHERINE'S HILL

Nowhere in Winchester better illustrates the change of seasons through the year than the water meadows. These have been preserved as an Area of Outstanding Natural Beauty by virtue of being the flood plain of the Itchen's wide valley bottom. Little of it is suitable for building on, as the Cathedral found to its cost.

A mizmaze was cut around 1700 near the twelfth-century Chapel of St Catherine, built in the centre of the copse of beech trees (once known locally as the Clump), on the summit of St Catherine's Hill. There is still plenty of unresolved speculation about the purpose of the mizmaze, which can be clearly seen in front of the spectacular copse, although no trace remains of the Chapel. Many believe that the origin of the mizmaze lies in penitential ritual; others think that its use was more recreational, as at 624 metres/2,047 feet in length and cut from nine 'nested' squares, its design is similar to the pattern used for playing the old English country game called Nine Men's Morris. The Iron Age people who lived here over 2,500 years ago built a fort on the summit to take advantage of the steep slopes and panoramic views. They hoarded grain within the walls of the fort and reared livestock in the fields below.

In 1666 plague pits were dug in the valley south of St Catherine's Hill in which to dispose of the city's dead. Around 160 years ago there was a water-powered saw mill on the Itchen Navigation Canal at the foot of the hill, some remains of which can be seen today. From St Catherine's Hill there are spectacular views of the city, the Cathedral, the College, St Cross and the lovely water meadows that fill the valley floor, with the Itchen flowing through them. The water meadows are one of Winchester's greatest assets, and they can be explored by a network of footpaths that ring the valley and divert to the summit of the hill and through a nature reserve.

PAGES 74–75 Looking north to St Catherine's Hill
over the old plague pits
FAR LEFT The water meadows
LEFT View to St Catherine's Hill
PAGES 78–79 The Itchen flowing through the water meadows
close to the city centre, in winter

Winter views of the Itchen
Navigation Canal

TOP Boys from Winchester College rowing on the Itchen Navigation
BOTTOM The banks of the Itchen, bursting into life in spring

The magnificent wing nut trees in full summer bloom in the water meadows nature reserve

Houses on the banks of the
Itchen Navigation where it
enters the water meadows

The ancient copse and the mizmaze on St Catherine's Hill, through the seasons

The Walled City and the Suburbs

THE WALLED CITY AND THE SUBURBS

Winchester has distinctive areas of urban settlement that have evolved as a consequence of its history and geography. The old Walled City includes the High Street, the Square, the Little and Great Minsters, the Broadway, Jewry, St Swithun's, Colebrook and St Thomas Streets, and the Law Courts, Barracks and Castle areas. These were all once surrounded by defensive walls, some of which remain today.

Immediately beyond the southern wall are Kingsgate and St Cross, with Oram's Arbour and West Hill to the west, Hyde to the north and the Soke and St Giles's Hill to the east, all of which can be considered suburbs of the walled city. Each has its share of the iconic buildings and interesting historical details that characterize the city.

This chapter is a visual record of the best of these buildings and details, captured at various times of the year.

The Walled City

By the Middle Ages the Norman palace built by William I in the L-shaped Square was gone and replaced by a thriving cattle and farmers' market. This was also the site of a pillory and whipping post and a place of public executions, which were announced by the tolling of the bell in the Church of St Lawrence-in-the-Square. This fifteenth-century church was also where bishops designate were obliged to robe and 'ring themselves in' before proceeding to the Cathedral. On these occasions people gathered to listen to the number of bell tolls, which denoted the number of years the new bishop intended to be head of the diocese. Today St Lawrence is almost hidden by offices and shops, with only its doorway visible to the public, and the Square is the location of Winchester's most interesting shops and café society. John Keats stayed in a room above what is now the stylish Cadogan clothes shop during his time in the city. The next-door delicatessen and pavement café makes the best cappuccinos in town. The brilliant City Museum now occupies the old Market House opposite the Eclipse, one of the oldest pubs in the city.

PAGES 86–87 City Bridge and the Weirs
FAR LEFT Great Minster Street leading to the Square
LEFT Castle Hill

TOP St Swithun-upon-Kingsgate
BOTTOM The Old Guildhall Clock in the High Street

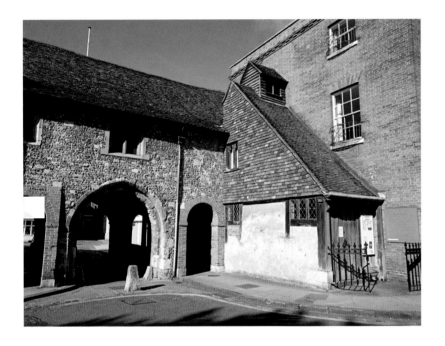

Winchester's other unusual church, St Swithun-upon-Kingsgate, surmounting the historic gateway, is also still used for regular services. The sanctity provided by this utterly charming place of worship has ensured the preservation of the ancient Kingsgate below. The gateway is now closed to traffic in order to maintain the peaceful nature of this very special historic corner of the city but remains an important pedestrian thoroughfare, linking the Cathedral Close and St Swithun's Street to the Kingsgate 'village', formed by College, Cannon and Kingsgate Streets.

The walled city's original Guildhall (now a branch of Lloyds Bank) was rebuilt in 1713, with the addition of a statue of Queen Anne, in a failed bid to reinstate Winchester as a royal city. The ornate clock that hangs on a bracket above the High Street is a replica of the one that rang a curfew call at eight o'clock every weekday evening to indicate the time to extinguish all home fires. This tradition is still maintained today. A flamboyant Gothic-revival-style Guildhall was constructed in 1873 on the Broadway, close to the ruins of Nunnaminster and the eighteenth-century Abbey House and Gardens, which today are the official residence of the Mayor of Winchester and a city park.

The Buttercross erected in the fifteenth century on the High Street is today regarded as the city's centre and is a popular meeting place. The origins of its name are unclear; theories range from it being the only place during Lent where butter could be consumed to it being the place where butter was sold at medieval farmers' markets. When a local landlord called Thomas Dummer attempted to purchase the cross and relocate it in his grounds in 1770, Wintonians organized a small riot and forced his workmen to abandon their attempt to dismantle it.

Also found in the High Street is God Begot House, a fine timber structure that was once a sanctuary for lawbreakers. Down a passage beside it is the Royal Oak, a pub that claims to have the oldest bar in England. The Pentice, an atmospheric covered walkway along the High Street, was created by extending the upper floors of the sixteenth-century timber-framed houses, which are now occupied by shops.

Jewry Street, which runs north from the High Street, was once the city's Jewish quarter and is now home to a collection of shops, offices, restaurants and bars, as well as the Winchester Discovery Centre, a library and exhibition space housed in the old Corn Exchange.

LEFT The Guildhall
RIGHT The Buttercross

TOP God Begot House
BOTTOM The Discovery Centre
and the former Corn Exchange on
Jewry Street

TOP The nineteenth-century Abbey House, the official residence of the Mayor
BOTTOM Abbey Gardens, a city centre public park with a stream of the Itchen

LEFT The Friends Meeting House in Colebrook Street

Kingsgate Village at dusk
TOP LEFT The Kingsgate Books & Prints shop, under Kingsgate
TOP RIGHT Kingsgate Road
BOTTOM LEFT The corner of Kingsgate Road and College Street
BOTTOM RIGHT The Wykeham Arms

Kingsgate and St Cross

This area has a particularly impressive share of Winchester's antiquities because of the dominance of the Cathedral and College. Between them they have owned a large proportion of the local buildings for centuries, saving them from replacement or modernization. As well as a host of period timber-framed and stone-built residential properties this area is home to some of Winchester's most interesting shops.

Under the arch of Kingsgate itself is the bow-windowed Kingsgate Books and Prints, selling a fascinating collection of vintage images and records of the city. On the corner of Kingsgate and Canon Streets is the Wykeham Arms, one of the oldest Inns in England, decorated with eclectic memorabilia from Britain's Imperial past and furnished with old desks from Winchester College. Opposite it is Kingsgate Wines and Provisions, a traditional-style provisions store and wine merchant that by default acts as a tuck shop for College boys. It is still known locally as 'the PO' on account of it having once been the village post office. Cornflowers, a shop that sells everything from modern designer goods to children's toys and birthday cards, occupies one of the most enviable locations in the neighbourhood behind a row of elegant sash windows on the corner of Kingsgate and College Streets. At one end of it is a window-mounted Victorian post box with its original enamelled sign that is still used for daily collections of mail.

Further down College Street is the art nouveau-fronted P&G Wells Bookshop. There has been a bookseller's and binder's here for nearly three hundred years, once supplying all the books, pens and ink for the College. Wykehamists still come here to order and collect their course books and a bookbinder's workshop still operates behind the shop. A few doors down at No. 8 is the house that the novelist Jane Austen moved to from the Hampshire village of Chawton when she became ill in May 1817 to be near the Winchester doctor who was treating her; she succumbed to Addison's disease aged forty-one on 18 July. Her funeral was held in Winchester Cathedral.

LEFT Looking north along Kingsgate Road
CENTRE TOP Blossom on College Street
CENTRE BOTTOM The west side of Kingsgate Road
BELOW The Old Pump House on Garnier Road

ABOVE A Christmas wreath on a door in Back Street
RIGHT Back Street in the snow

Hyde

Apart from a fifteenth-century gatehouse, nothing of Hyde Abbey remains; once its tower and spire would have dominated the skyline in the way that the church of St Cross Hospital does today. But there are later buildings of historical relevance that have survived in Hyde. These include Hyde Tavern, a truly old-style 'wet' pub in a fine building, which serves plenty of good ales but no food; the Dutch brick gabled Hyde House; the eighteenth-century Hyde Abbey House, which was once a school; and St Bartholomew's Church, one of only four medieval parish churches in Winchester today (along with the churches of St John, St Lawrence and St Swithun) and still used for regular worship.

TOP The Hyde Tavern in Hyde Street
BOTTOM   Hyde House, with its Dutch brick gable

TOP LEFT Hyde Abbey Gate
BOTTOM LEFT St Batholomew's Church
RIGHT The old boundary wall in Hyde

TOP The Black Boy in Wharf Hill
BOTTOM A surviving stretch of the old city walls, beside the Itchen

The Soke and St Giles's Hill

The area to east of the Broadway and Wolvesey Palace, including Wharf Hill, St Giles's Hill, Chesil Street, Water Lane and Magdalen Hill, is collectively known as the Soke. This was the area of Winchester that came under the jurisdiction of the resident bishop rather than the city. Winchester's medieval bishops wielded tremendous power from the fortified and moated Wolvesey and were free to collect their own taxes from the residents and merchants of the Soke. During the annual fortnight's fair on St Giles's Hill all other commerce was banned and the mayor was obliged to hand over the keys of the city to the Bishop, who collected substantial fees from the stallholders.

Even today the Bishop has his own exclusive and private access to the Cathedral via a secret doorway that links the grounds of Wolvesey Palace to the back of Cathedral Close. The numbers of relics from the past that still survive in the Soke are not quite on a par with those of Kingsgate but come a close second.

Wharf Hill is reached from Wolvesey via Black Bridge, built so that the bishops could cross the Itchen and have access to the Palace without having to enter the city. Beyond the very grand Black Bridge House are a row of charming bargee's cottages, built to accommodate families of the men who operated the trade of coal and goods transported by barge up from Southampton Water, until the railway replaced the canal in 1869.

Near the top of the hill is the Black Boy pub, a converted stone and flint stable block with a fine collection of local ales, famously relaxed atmosphere and regular live music events, including some excellent impromptu gatherings of Irish folk musicians. Across the road on the corner with Chesil Street is the splendid Michelin-starred restaurant the Black Rat.

The water meadows that stretch all the way from beyond St Cross right into the old city at Black Bridge are joined to the equally rural Winnal Moors Nature Reserve to the north, via Weirs Walk (along which there are still remnants of the city's Roman walls), City Bridge and Water Lane. Above Water Lane, Blue Ball Hill leads steeply up to St John's Street and Beggars Lane. Around this junction is an interesting collection of well-preserved buildings, including the fourteenth-century Blue Boar House with an unusual overhanging first floor, and the last remaining stable block in Winchester at St John's Croft. St John's Church itself, founded in 1193, is one of the most interesting in the city, with a fine rood screen and an arched recess containing an altar tomb. It was used by the scholars of the College while they waited for their own chapel to be built.

TOP The medieval stone wall
along the east bank of the Itchen
BOTTOM A private bridge
over the Itchen, belonging to
Kingsland House

LEFT The fourth-century Blue Boar House
RIGHT Beggars Lane
BELOW Spring blossom in Wharf Hill

LEFT Christ Church West Hill
TOP RIGHT Pagoda House on St James' Lane
BOTTOM RIGHT Clifton House in Oram's Arbour

Oram's Arbour and West Hill

Today Oram's Arbour is an upmarket residential area of leafy avenues and grand houses, built around an open area of grassland used as a city park. West Hill also has many fine houses up on St James' Lane, overlooking the cemetery of Christ Church and St Catherine's Hill.

The tree-lined west side of Oram's Arbour

A Year of
City Events

A YEAR OF CITY EVENTS

Christmas and mid-summer are the highlights of the year in Winchester, although there is usually something interesting going on somewhere at any time. In the weeks leading up to Christmas a large market and an ice rink are set up in the Cathedral Close, creating a very festive atmosphere. On Christmas Eve a brass band plays by the Buttercross in the High Street and the boy choristers from Pilgrims' School are invited into the Wykeham Arms Inn to sing carols in front of roaring fires. All summer there are open-air festivals of music, food, dance and drama, and in July Britain's longest-running festival of street theatre, the Hat Fair (so named as people throw money into the hats of the performers), is held over a long weekend.

Being a city with a long military tradition, Remembrance Day is a big affair in Winchester, with a parade of marching bands through the streets on their way to the service at the Cathedral, where a lone trumpeter delivers the Last Post. Winchester is also a legal city with a Crown Court, which is celebrated annually by a service in the Cathedral attended by all the dignitaries from the Court, dressed in their traditional robes and finery.

Twice every month the normally bland part of the town along the Brooks and a nearby car park are transformed into a feast of fresh farm produce and food stalls by the Hampshire Farmers' Market. It is always a joy to shop there for a fantastic variety of the best-quality vegetables, meat, cheese, fish and fruit, all from the local area, and meet the people who produce it.

PAGES 110–111 The annual gathering of the Law Courts at the Cathedral, on Law Sunday
FAR LEFT The winter ice rink in the Cathedral Close
LEFT The Christmas Market in the Cathedral Close

Seasonal produce on sale at the Hampshire
Farmers' Market held in Winchester on two
Sundays of every month

Street performers at the annual Hat Fair

The Summer Fête at St Cross

LEFT Law Sunday at the Cathedral
BELOW Remembrance Day

My Winchester

MY WINCHESTER

I spent much of my youth in Winchester without really appreciating what a unique and special place it was. As is often the case, it was only after leaving – to spend thirty years away travelling the world and staying up in London between trips – and then returning that I began to discover its many qualities. I started with weekend visits that soon became more frequent and longer, and I have now returned to live there full time. I celebrate that privilege every day.

I try to start every day with a morning walk in the water meadows. These are always best when taken at dawn, which is not always possible, but it is always worth the effort when it is, even if in mid-summer it means starting ridiculously early. There is hardly ever anyone else around at dawn – an occasional dog walker at most – so it is a brilliant time to see wildlife. Deer, heron, water voles are all regular sightings along with the obvious rabbits, ducks and swans; birds like kingfishers and water rails less so and otters hardly ever, although they are always there.

Even a short walk around the small nature reserve near the College is rewarding. This can be achieved in less than twenty minutes.

A longer route continues to include a climb to the summit of St Catherine's Hill, from where the view is different every day and the copse enchanting. Descending straight down the steep bank to the south and climbing up the other side of a valley full of rabbit warrens, a path leads to Five Bridges Road, which crosses the many channels of the Itchen to the west. At the other end a path across farmland on the right leads to the avenue of limes next to St Cross. It follows the Itchen past an old water mill and pump station, and then past the idyllic College sports grounds along a section of river that is home to several water voles, before ending in College Street next to the nature reserve again. This walk takes at least two hours, all in beautiful countryside (except for a few glimpses of the M3), and can be made without even leaving the city. It is never dull, as even in bad weather that would be nothing but tiresome and unwelcome in an urban setting there is a sense of drama in the wide open space. On fine days at any time of the year the walk is a pure joy and the best

way to start any day. At some times of the year things slow down and the only changes from day to day are almost too subtle to notice; at others the landscape and natural habitat seem to change radically overnight.

The path up to the viewpoint on St Giles's Hill is not quite as bucolic but worth taking for the view of the whole city spread out right beneath the hill. It looks west straight up the Broadway, over the statue of King Alfred, into the High Street and on up to Westgate, with a bird's-eye view of the Cathedral and College on the left. It is particularly fine on a bright winter morning with the sun behind you and minimum foliage to obstruct the view.

The city's other magnificent view is looking north from Bushfield Down in summer, when the only buildings visible above the treeline are the towers of St Cross, the College Chapel and the Cathedral, with nothing but open farmland stretching to the horizon behind them.

The most perfect day possible in Winchester is a long walk in fine weather on one of the Sundays when the Hampshire Farmers' Market is in town. It is the biggest and best farmers' market in England and one of the most important things that contribute to making living in Winchester or a visit such a special experience. Every farmer, cheese maker, butcher, baker, fishmonger, wine maker, brewer, cake baker, egg seller and soup seller there is from Hampshire or within 16 kilometres / 10 miles of its borders, so all the produce is as fresh as it is possible to be. Even better, you get the chance to buy it direct from the people who grew, reared, baked, brewed or made it. Shopping for food here is a complete pleasure and the produce so fresh that it easily lasts until the next market two weeks later. Like walking in the water meadows, shopping in the market keeps you totally in tune with the seasons. You always feel a ripple of excitement when a new vegetable such as broad beans or asparagus comes into season and is back on sale after a long absence. The produce is much more exotic than just cabbage and potatoes and includes locally grown things like Chinese water spinach, jalapeño chillies and pak choi. There are even water buffalo burgers on sale.

An evening walk through the Kingsgate 'village' area of Winchester always makes me feel as if I am holiday: it's like walking back into the past in the way that visiting a Tuscan hill village or a Provençal hamlet is, but a completely English version of it. The cobbled winding streets of timber-framed houses, the architectural splendour of the College and the antiquity of the gateway and the church perched above it combine to create a seductive atmosphere,

PAGES 120–121 The copse on St Catherine's Hill, at sunrise on a misty winter morning
LEFT One of the wild deer that roam the water meadows, on a frosty morning

TOP LEFT The Hampshire Farmers' Market in summer
BOTTOM LEFT Cadogan on the Square
TOP RIGHT Kingsgate village at dusk
BOTTOM RIGHT Inside the Wykeham Arms

especially at night, when there is almost no one around. It is also essential to come here during the day to buy books at the excellent P&G Wells Bookshop. There is always a warm welcome at the Wykeham Arms, which still serves the favourite Hampshire ale of my youth, HSB (Horndean Special Bitter). Although it is now made in London by Fuller's, it still has a taste full of pleasure and nostalgia. This is the most civilized and genteel pub in the city, oozing with old world tradition, with charming and exceptionally polite staff, roaring fires in winter and a sunny summer garden. The walls and ceilings are covered in an eclectic collection of vintage paintings, posters, obscure objects and bizarre memorabilia. Best of all, a pot full of home-cooked bangers is placed on the bar at six o'clock every evening.

The other great hostelry in the city is the Black Boy, just over the Black Bridge on the other side of the Itchen, a little way up Wharf Hill. This is also a place of roaring winter fires and a sunny summer garden, but the eclectic memorabilia here is much more eccentric, the atmosphere more relaxed and even a little bohemian. There is an excellent range of Hampshire ales, table football, board games and live music. A couple of Monday evenings a month a random collection of Irish folk musicians gather to play anything from improvised jams to traditional ballads. It's all a bit vague, but when it comes together it can be brilliant.

One of the things I like best about Winchester is that just as accessible as all the nature and tradition are elements of a thoroughly modern city. I enjoy a cappuccino and croissant on the pavement café tables of Cadogan & James in the Square as much as I did in any trendy Soho café. The clothes on sale in the Cadogan shop next door are as cool and sophisticated as any I have found in a cutting-edge Chelsea boutique. The Screen Cinema shows art house films on Tuesday nights, and the Michelin-starred Black Rat (same owners as the Black Boy and Winchester's coolest wine bar, the Black Bottle) on Chesil Street rivals any restaurant I have eaten in anywhere.

I would never miss the wonderful experience of attending the Christmas Eve midnight service in the Cathedral and I can't resist frequent visits to the crypt every winter to see if it has flooded. I love the view of the Cathedral from the garden of the Friends Meeting House and the house itself is one of the most attractive in the city. My highlights of any year in Winchester are the pomp and ceremony of any event in the Cathedral, the timeless charm of the

St Cross Fête, the constantly changing natural rhythms of the water meadows, the mystical atmosphere of the copse on St Catherine's Hill, the day broad beans arrive in the farmers' market and New Year's Eve in the Black Boy.

Another very significant part of the pleasure of living in Winchester is the easy access to other places. London is only an hour away by train and not much more by car, depending on time of travel. Far more importantly, the fabulous countryside of Hampshire is right on the doorstep. Walks along the upper Itchen, Test and Meon valleys, up Winchester and Beacon Hills or among the idyllic Hampshire Hangers around Selbourne are only a short drive away. Nearby National Trust properties such as Hinton Ampner and Mottisfont (which has a fabulous walled rose garden) are straight out of a Jane Austen novel.

Winchester is a hard place to hide, being so near to London and just off the M3, but it is also easy to miss, being tucked into the Itchen valley and so full of trees. I am very glad I have found it again. There is an avenue of huge old wingnut trees along a small brook between the Itchen and the canal that I think is the most perfect place on earth, where I want my ashes scattered.

The brook that runs past the avenue of wingnut trees in the water meadows

INDEX Page numbers in *italics* refer to illustrations.